Contents

Rolling, Sliding, and Sticking 29

Balancing, Swinging, and Spinning 47

Throwing, Flying, and Falling 63

Floating, Bouncing, and Pushing 81

Plucking, Banging, and Blowing 97

Introduction

Toys are fun, but you probably never thought they could teach you about science. Well, they can, if you use the activities in this book. Why does your Slinky slink down the steps? Why does a swing go higher when you pump it? And when you flip your Etch-A-Sketch over, why is your picture erased?

Science in Seconds with Toys will help you find the answers. After experimenting with the toys in this book, study your other toys and think about what science concepts are behind the way they work. Before you know it, you'll have them all figured out, you'll ace your next science test, and maybe even come up with ideas for new toys.

HOW THE BOOK IS ORGANIZED

Science in Seconds with Toys is divided into sections by what the toy does (bouncing, floating, etc.). Each experiment provides a question about a toy, a list of materials you'll need, easy-to-follow steps, and an explanation of the conclusion of the experiment. All of the materials are readily available, and the process for completing the experiments is safe, easy to follow, and fun. Each experiment takes only about 10 minutes or less to complete. So what are you waiting for? Grab that Silly Putty and let's go!

REFLECTING, REFRACTING, AND GLOWING

PRISM INSPECTION

How Does a Prism Make Rainbows?

MATERIALS

prism

Note: This experiment should be performed on a sunny day.

PROCEDURE

1. Lay the prism directly in the sunlight on a table or other surface.
2. Look at the reflections of light on the surface near the prism.

EXPLANATION

You could see all of the colors of the rainbow on the surface near the prism. What we see as white light is actually a mixture of rainbow colors called the **spectrum.** A **prism** is a clear solid triangular figure that bends the light rays of each color a little differently so you can see the color separately.

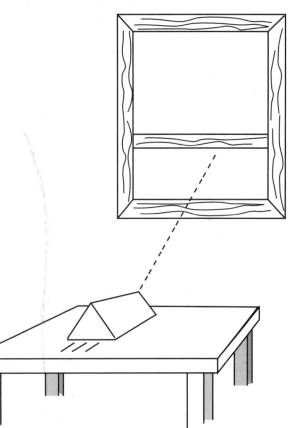

BUBBLE STUDY

What Do the Colors in a Bubble Reveal?

MATERIALS

bubble blower
bubble solution
outdoor area

*Note: This experiment should be performed
on a sunny day.*

PROCEDURE

1. Dip the bubble blower in the solution.
2. Blow some bubbles.
3. Closely examine the bubbles in the light.

EXPLANATION

When you studied the bubbles, you saw all of the colors of the rainbow. These colors come from white light, which is made up of rays of different wave-lenghths. (A **wavelength** is the direction of movement of a wave.) When light hits the water in the bubble, it is split up into its different wavelengths, which you see as rainbow colors. The liquid bubble film flows and swirls, changing in thickness and color.

COLOR CUES

Why Are Objects of the Same Color Sometimes Difficult to See?

MATERIALS

tape
sheet of construction paper the
    same color as one of the cars
toy cars in several colors
yardstick (meterstick)

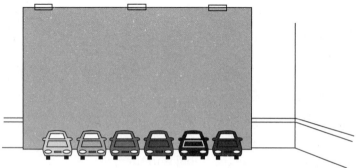

PROCEDURE

1. Tape the sheet of construction paper to a wall.
2. Line up all of the cars in front of the sheet of construction paper.
3. Stand about 5 feet (1.5 meters) away from the cars and the construction paper. Which car is the hardest to see?

EXPLANATION

The car that was the same color as the construction paper was the hardest to see. Your eyes see color because of **reflected** (bounced back) light. When you see a lot of reflected light of the same color, it's hard to distinguish specific shapes. A blue car looks like part of blue paper, until your brain tells your eyes to look again more closely at more subtle variations in color. Some animals are able to change colors to match their backgrounds. This is called **camouflage.** Animals use camouflage to hide from their enemies.

LARGER LOOK

How Does a Magnifying Lens Work?

MATERIALS

magnifying lens
small object

PROCEDURE

1. Hold the lens and the small object close to your eye and view the object through the lens.
2. Move the object, but not the lens, farther away from your face. What happens?

EXPLANATION

When you held the object close to your eye, it was one size. When you moved it away, it appeared much larger. It looked larger because the **magnifying lens** (piece of glass that makes objects look larger) increases the angle at which your eye sees the object. The lens bends the light rays coming from the object. **Magnification** is the process of making objects look larger by passing light from an object through a lens. A magnifying lens uses **convex lenses** (pieces of glass that are thicker in the middle than at the edges) to bend the light rays.

GLOW IN THE DARK

What Causes Some Paints and Objects to Glow in the Dark?

MATERIALS

paintbrush
glow-in-the-dark paints
paper
scissors
masking tape

*Note: Ask permission from an
adult to tape these stars
to your ceiling.*

PROCEDURE

1. Paint some stars on the paper with the glow-in-the-dark paint.
2. Cut out the stars.
3. Put tape on the backs of the stars and press them onto the wall.
4. Turn off the lights and look at the wall.

EXPLANATION

The stars glowed in the dark. The glow-in-the-dark paints have a chemical in them that can take in energy from light. In the dark, the paints give off or release the light energy. Materials that give off light energy after the source of energy has been turned off are called **phosphorescent.**

COLORED GLASSES

How Do Three-Dimensional (3-D) Glasses Work?

MATERIALS

3-D comic book
3-D glasses

PROCEDURE

1. Look at the book without the glasses on.
2. Now put the glasses on and look at the book. What happens?

EXPLANATION

Without the glasses, you saw flat, blurry pictures. When you put the glasses on and looked at the book, the figures and characters seemed to jump off the page. They looked three-dimensional. A two-dimensional object is totally flat. It only has height and width. But a three-dimensional object also has depth. You are able to see objects as 3-D because your eyes are slightly separated. Each eye sees a slightly different picture. Try closing one eye at a time, and you'll see how this works. Your brain puts the two pictures together and you see three-dimensional objects! This is called **stereoscopic vision.** A 3-D picture is actually flat, but it has one picture for the right eye and a slightly different picture for the left eye. The colored lenses in the glasses keep each eye from seeing the other eye's picture. Your brain combines the two pictures to show you one 3-D image.

SHADOW PUPPETS

Why Do Shadows Change Size?

MATERIALS

yardstick (meterstick)
white wall
flashlight
your hand

PROCEDURE

1. Place a table about 6 feet (2 m) from the wall.
2. Turn the flashlight on and lay it on the table so that the light shines on the wall.
3. Hold your hand about 1 foot (30 cm) away from the wall so its shadow falls on the wall. Study the shadow.
4. Walk 2 feet (60 cm) away from the wall. Now look at the shadow. How is this shadow different from the first one?

EXPLANATION

When you held your hand in front of the light, you made a shadow on the wall. When your hand was closer to the light, the shadow was larger and less distinct than when your hand was farther away. The hand blocks more light the closer it is to the source. Because light bends around edges of objects, the edges of the shadow from the hand closer to the light were more blurry.

SWIMMING GOGGLES

Why Do Swimming Goggles Help You See Better Underwater?

MATERIALS

swimming pool or beach
swimming goggles

Note: Be sure the pool or beach is supervised by a lifeguard.

PROCEDURE

1. Hold your breath and duck underwater. Open your eyes and look around.
2. Put the swimming goggles over your eyes. Look around underwater again. What do you notice?

EXPLANATION

The **cornea** (outer layer) of your eye must **refract** (bend) light rays in order for you to see a clear image on your **retina** (the inner layer of lining of the eyeball that reacts to light). If water is covering your eye, nearly all that ability to refract is lost. If you wear goggles, the layer of air in front of your eyes gives your eyes normal refraction. Fish see better underwater than you do because they have two retinas in each eye.

VIEW-MASTER® VIEWER

How Do Three-Dimensional Objects Appear in a View-Master?

MATERIALS

View-Master film wheel
View-Master

PROCEDURE

1. Examine the View-Master film wheel by holding it up to the light.
2. Put the film wheel in the View-Master.
3. Turn the wheel and look at the film through the viewer.

EXPLANATION

The pictures appear to be three-dimensional. A View-Master is really a **stereoscope.** The pictures on the film show the same picture from two different angles. When you looked in the eyeholes, your brain combined the two flat images into a single three-dimensional image. Because of the position of your eyes on your head, each eye sees everything from a slightly different angle.

PERISCOPE PEEPING

How Does a Periscope Let You See around Corners?

MATERIALS

periscope

PROCEDURE

1. Hold the periscope up to your face.
2. Look through the eyehole at the mirror in the bottom of the periscope. What do you see?
3. Turn the periscope to the side and look through the eyehole. What do you see?
4. Think of ways you can use the periscope.

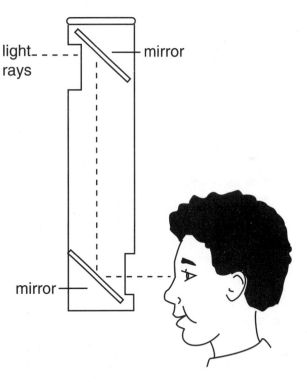

EXPLANATION

A **periscope** is a tube-shaped instrument with angled mirrors inside it. The top mirror catches the image of an object and reflects the image at a right angle into another mirror at the other end of the tube. The second mirror reflects the image at a right angle into your eyes. You can take a periscope to a parade to see over people. Or you can use it to look over a fence and around corners.

KALEIDOSCOPE PATTERNS

How Does a Kaleidoscope Work?

MATERIALS

3 pocket mirrors
masking tape
small toys, game pieces, and bits of colored
    paper

PROCEDURE

1. Stand the 3 mirrors on their ends, facing one another, to form a triangle.
2. Tape the mirrors together.
3. Stand the mirrors on a table.
4. Put the small toys, game pieces, and bits of paper in the space between the mirrors.
5. Look straight down into the mirrors. What do you see?

EXPLANATION

Each object seems to be multiplied. By putting the 3 mirrors together, you created a kaleidoscope. A **kaleidoscope** is a long tube containing mirrors that cause multiple reflections. Kaleidoscopes usually have pieces of brightly colored objects at one end and an eyehole at the other. When you look in the eyehole, you see light rays from the objects reflecting back and forth between the mirrors. Each object is repeated, making interesting patterns.

OPERATION® GAME

How Does an Electric Current Work?

MATERIALS

Operation game with battery

PROCEDURE

1. Turn on the game.
2. Use the tweezers to try and take the small piece out of a space without touching the side of the hole. What happens if you hit the side of the hole with the tweezers?

EXPLANATION

The patient's nose lights up if you hit the side of the hole with the tweezers. The game Operation® uses the path of an electric current, and this path is called a **circuit.** The electric circuit flows from the battery, through the metal surrounding the hole, to the lightbulb in the nose, and back to the battery. If the tweezers touch the metal, the circuit becomes complete. Completing the circuit causes the light in the nose to light up.

MIXING, MOLDING, AND STRETCHING

PAINT WITH WATER

What Causes the Color to Come Out in Paint-with-Water Books?

MATERIALS

permanent marker
sheet of paper
2 paintbrushes: 1 thick, 1 thin
watercolor paints
bowl of clean water

PROCEDURE

1. With the permanent marker, draw the outline of a shape such as a circle on the paper.
2. Dip the thin paint brush into the watercolor paints.
3. Using only the very tip of the brush, make very tiny dots to fill in the shape you have drawn. Make as many dots as you can without any dot touching another dot.
4. Let the paint dry.
5. Dip the thicker brush into the bowl of clean water.
6. Using the thicker brush, wipe water across the dots. What happens?

EXPLANATION

When you used the wet brush on the paint dots, you spread the color out to fill in the shape. The ink used in paint-with-water books is a special kind of ink that dissolves and runs when water touches it. This kind of paint is called water-soluble paint. Any substance that dissolves in water is **soluble.** The ink used to draw the outline of the shape is permanent because it does not dissolve in water.

DRYING PAINT

Why Does Paint on a Picture Dry?

MATERIALS

paintbrush
cup of water
watercolor paints
paper

PROCEDURE

1. Dip the paintbrush into the cup of water.
2. Dip the wet paintbrush into one of the paints and swirl it around.
3. Paint a picture on the paper.
4. Put your painting in a place where it won't be disturbed.
5. From time to time, examine the picture to see the paint dry.

EXPLANATION

The paint dried when the water evaporated. **Evaporation** is the process by which a liquid turns into a gas. When you swirled the wet brush in the paint, you mixed the colored paint with the water. The paint was transferred to the paper in the water, then left on the paper when the water evaporated.

PERSONALIZED PAINT

How Can You Make Your Own Paint?

MATERIALS

knife (to be used only by an adult)
adult helper
beet
jar with lid
¼ cup (60 ml) water
strainer
empty margarine container
3 tablespoons (45 ml) white paint
craft stick

PROCEDURE

1. Ask an adult to cut the beet into tiny pieces.
2. Put the pieces of beet in the jar.
3. Pour the water into the jar. Screw the lid on the jar tightly and shake the jar.
4. Put the strainer over the margarine container.
5. Unscrew the lid of the jar and pour the beets and the water into the strainer.
6. Remove the strainer and throw the beet pieces away.
7. Add the white paint to the beet juice.
8. Use the craft stick to mix the white paint and the beet juice together. What color do you have?

EXPLANATION

When you mixed the red beet juice with the white paint, you created pink paint. Beets have a red pigment in them. **Pigments** are complex substances that give objects their colors. A pigment produces a certain color by reflecting only some wavelengths of light. When you see a red object, such as the beet, you are actually seeing the color red reflected off the object. You used a natural pigment for your paint. These days most pigments are man-made.

COLORED MARKERS

What Makes Up the Colors in Colored Markers?

MATERIALS

water-based markers: purple, brown, green,
and orange
paper towels
empty jar without lid
eyedropper or straw
cup of water

PROCEDURE

1. Use one color of marker to make a colored circle in the center of a paper towel.
2. Lay the paper towel over the mouth of the jar.
3. Suction a few drops of water from the cup with the eyedropper.
4. Release 2 or 3 drops of water onto the colored circle. Watch what happens.
5. Repeat steps 1 to 4 with the remaining colored markers.

EXPLANATION

Colored dyes and inks are made by mixing two or more **primary colors** (red, blue, and yellow) together. **Chromatography** is a method of separating mixed colors into primary colors. When you dropped the water onto the colored circle, the colors it was made of separated out. For example, a green mark would have separated into yellow and blue.

CHALK FIZZ

How Can You Make Chalk Fizz?

MATERIALS

chalk
saucer
eyedropper
vinegar

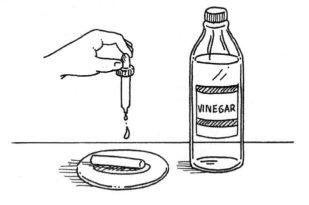

PROCEDURE

1. Put the chalk in the saucer
2. Dip the eyedropper in the vinegar.
3. Squeeze 3 or 4 small drops of vinegar onto the chalk. What happens?

EXPLANATION

When you put the vinegar on the chalk, the chalk gave off fizzy bubbles. Chalk is made from a rock called **limestone.** Limestone forms on the bottom of seas from ground-up seashells, which are made of **calcium carbonate.** Any substance containing a carbonate will dissolve if combined with an **acid** (a chemical compound that dissolves in water and tastes sour). Vinegar contains acetic acid, which reacted with the carbonate in the chalk by giving off bubbles of a gas called carbon dioxide.

SOAP BUBBLES

How Does Soap Make Bubbles?

MATERIALS

bubble blower
measuring cup
water
¼ cup (60 ml) Dawn dishwashing liquid
1 tablespoon (15 ml) glycerin
jar
spoon
outdoor area

PROCEDURE

1. Dip the bubble blower in ¼ cup (60 ml) of water.
2. Try to blow bubbles with the water. Can you blow bubbles?
3. Pour the dishwashing liquid, 2 cups (500 ml) of water, and the glycerin in the jar.
4. Mix the dishwashing liquid, water, and glycerin with the spoon very slowly.
5. Use the bubble blower to blow bubbles with the bubble solution you have made.

EXPLANATION

It is not possible to blow bubbles with plain water because of the water **molecules** (the smallest parts of a substance that have all the properties of the substance). The molecules in water have a strong attraction for each other. This makes water molecules cling together, especially at the surface. This is called **surface tension**. Soap weakens the pull of the water and makes the surface of the water much stretchier. Instead of breaking, the solution stretches enough for you to blow air inside it. Glycerin makes the bubbles last longer.

STRETCHY BALLOON

Why Do Balloons Stretch?

MATERIALS

mirror
balloon

PROCEDURE

1. Stand in front of the mirror.
2. Blow up the balloon. What do you notice as you are blowing air into the balloon?
3. Let the air out of the balloon. What happens?

EXPLANATION

Balloons are made from a gooey material called **latex,** which comes from plants. Latex is very elastic. **Elastic** materials are easily stretched and return to their original shape. When you blew into the balloon, you pushed air into it and stretched the latex. When you let the air out, the balloon returned to its original shape.

TWO BALLOONS

Why Do Balloons Made of Mylar® Float Longer Than Latex Balloons?

MATERIALS

helium-filled Mylar balloon
helium-filled latex balloon

PROCEDURE

1. Examine the Mylar and the latex balloons. Note the similarities and the differences.
2. Put the balloons in an area where they can remain untouched for 2 days.
3. Check the balloons after 2 days. Which is still floating?

EXPLANATION

Helium is a tasteless, colorless, odorless gas that is lighter than air. When helium is put into a balloon, the balloon will float. As we saw in the previous experiment, latex stretches easily. When the latex balloon stretches, the spaces between the latex molecules allow tiny amounts of the helium to escape. In **Mylar,** a man-made polyester material made of very thin sheets, the **chemical bonds** (connections) between the molecules are much tighter. A Mylar balloon will hold helium and other gases a lot longer than a latex balloon. But even Mylar eventually lets the helium escape.

FUNNY PUTTY

Is Silly Putty® a Solid or a Liquid?

Experiment with Silly Putty or make your own funny putty with this recipe:

MATERIALS

2 cups (500 ml) white glue
1 cup (250 ml) liquid starch
bowl
spoon
airtight container

PROCEDURE

1. Put the white glue and the liquid starch in the bowl.
2. Use the spoon to mix the glue and the starch together very well.
3. Experiment with this putty or with the store-bought Silly Putty.
4. When you are finished, store the funny putty in an airtight container.

EXPLANATION

Silly Putty and the funny putty you made are unusual materials. If you pull it quickly, it snaps. If you pull it slowly, it stretches. A material that behaves in some ways like a solid and in other ways like a liquid is known as a **non-Newtonian fluid.** There are very few substances on Earth that have these qualities.

PLAY PLUBBER

What Are Polymers?

MATERIALS

1 teaspoon (5 ml) borax
1 cup (250 ml) water
2 small bowls
spoon
2 tablespoons (30 ml) white glue
food coloring

PROCEDURE

1. Put the borax and the water in one of the bowls and stir with the spoon until dissolved.

2. Put the white glue into the other bowl and add 3 or 4 drops of food coloring.

3. Add 1 tablespoon (5 ml) of the borax-and-water mixture to the white-glue-and-food-coloring mixture and stir well with the spoon.

4. Take the mixture out of the bowl and knead it in your hands.

EXPLANATION

The substance you have made is like plastic. Plastics are made of long chains of molecules called **polymers.** When these polymer chains are joined, they become very strong. Plastics can be either hard, like a bicycle helmet, or flexible, like your plubber.

ROLLING, SLIDING, AND STICKING

FRICTION FLURRY

Why Will a Toy Car Roll Farther Than a Lump of Clay?

MATERIALS

toy car
lump of clay
large, smooth, flat board

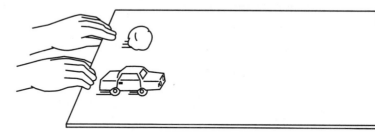

PROCEDURE

1. Place the toy car and the lump
    of clay side by side on one end of the board.
2. Slowly lift the end of the board where the objects are placed.
3. Watch the objects move down the board. Which goes faster and farther?

EXPLANATION

A toy car will roll faster and farther than a lump of clay because of friction.
Friction is the **force** (energy) that acts when two surfaces rub against one
another. Objects move faster and farther when there is less friction between
them and the surface they are on.

ROLLING BALL

How Does Surface Affect Movement?

MATERIALS

Ping-Pong ball
carpeted floor
wood floor

PROCEDURE

1. Holding the Ping-Pong ball at your waist, kneel on the carpeted floor and toss the ball. How far does it roll?
2. Move to the wood floor.
3. Hold the Ping-Pong ball at your waist and toss it. How far does it roll this time?

EXPLANATION

The Ping-Pong ball rolled farther on the wood floor than on the carpeted floor. Different surfaces have different amounts of friction. The more the friction, the more the ball will be slowed down. The carpeted surface offered much more friction than the wood floor, so it slowed the ball down more.

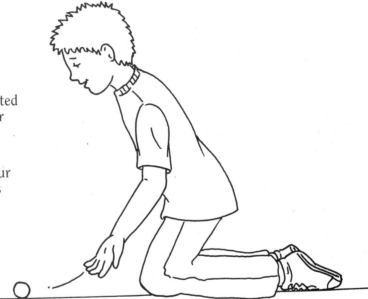

ROLLER SKATE ROLL

Why Do Roller Skates Roll So Smoothly?

MATERIALS

4 marbles

PROCEDURE

1. Open your hand and place it on a table or other flat surface.
2. Move your hand across the table.
3. Place 4 marbles on the table so that your open hand fits over them.
4. Slide your hand across the table, using the marbles as a base. What do you notice?

EXPLANATION

When you tried to slide your hand across the flat surface, your hand was slowed down by contact with the table. When you rolled your hand over the marbles, your hand moved much more easily. Rolling friction is less than sliding friction. The wheels of roller skates contain ball bearings, which are little, round, steel balls. Like the marble, these ball bearings help the wheels move smoothly by reducing friction.

MARBLE COLLISION

What Happens When One Marble Collides with a Line of Marbles?

MATERIALS

book
toy car track
7 marbles of the same size

PROCEDURE

1. Lay the book on one end of a table or other flat surface.
2. Put the pieces of car track together. Position the track so that one end lies flat at one side of the table and the other end rests on the book.
3. Line up 6 marbles on the flat end of the track so they touch each other.
4. Hold 1 marble at the raised end of the track and let it go. What happens?

EXPLANATION

The marble you let go collided with the first marble in the line. The marble at the end of the line was pushed from the track, but none of the other marbles moved. The **kinetic energy** (energy of a moving object) from the marble that hit the line of marbles was transferred through all of the marbles to the last one, which rolled away.

SOCCER PLAY

What Is the Best Way to Move a Soccer Ball Downfield?

MATERIALS

soccer ball
outdoor area
friend

PROCEDURE

1. With your friend, play a game of soccer outdoors using only the tip of your foot to move the ball around the field. Is this easy or difficult to do?

2. Now use the inside of your foot to move the ball. Is this a better way to move the ball?

EXPLANATION

When you moved the ball with your toes, it was very difficult to maneuver the ball. But when you used the inside of your foot, it was much easier to control the ball. This is because the inside of your foot has a larger surface area than your toes coming in contact with the ball.

ICE MELT

How Do Ice Skates Work?

MATERIALS

ice skates
ice rink

PROCEDURE

1. Put the ice skates on and skate around the rink. How does it feel?
2. Notice the trail your skates left on the ice.

EXPLANATION

You felt the skates gliding over the ice. When you ice-skate, your weight is concentrated on the blade of the skate. This creates **pressure** (the force placed on an object) under the blade. The pressure under the blade melts the ice a small amount and the blade slides across the thin layer of water created. After you pass, the water quickly refreezes, leaving a thin trail of new ice.

FASTER SKATING

How Can You Skate Faster?

MATERIALS

roller skates, in-line skates, or ice skates
skating surface

PROCEDURE

1. Put the skates on and skate standing
   up straight.
2. Now, lean forward as far as possible
   while skating. Do you go faster or slower?

EXPLANATION

When you bent over, you could go faster than when
you were standing up. When you try to skate very fast,
one thing that slows you down is the force of the air
pushing on your body. This force is called "air friction,"
or **drag.** The size of this drag depends on several things,
but the most important is the area of your body. When
you bend over, you reduce drag by making the area of
your body that hits the wind smaller. This is called
streamlining and it allows you to go faster.

SLICKY SLIDE

Why Does Waxed Paper Help You Move Down a Slide Faster?

MATERIALS

slide
waxed paper

PROCEDURE

1. Slide down the slide as you normally would.
2. Tear off a sheet of waxed paper slightly larger than your bottom.
3. Sit on the waxed paper and hold it with both hands at the top of the slide. Go down the slide with the waxed paper under your bottom. What was the difference in your sliding?

EXPLANATION

When you used the waxed paper, you slid faster than you did without it. Waxed paper is coated with a waxy substance that reduces friction. When you went down the slide the first time, your clothing slowed you down because it produced friction. Waxed paper reduced the amount of friction between you and the slide, so you went faster.

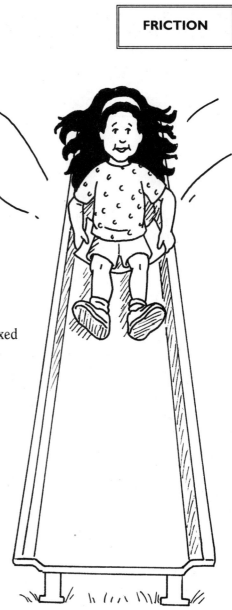

CHALK SCREECH

Why Does Writing with Chalk Sometimes Make Horrible Sounds?

MATERIALS

new box of chalk
chalkboard

PROCEDURE

1. Hold the chalk straight out from the board and write or draw. What happens?
2. Now hold the chalk at a slight angle to the board and write or draw.

EXPLANATION

When you wrote with the chalk sticking straight out from the board, it made a horrible sound. But when you held it at an angle, it did not make that sound. The chalk held straight out from the board produced more friction because more of the surface of the chalk was touching the board. The friction made the chalk and the board move back and forth very quickly and give off a sound. You can make the same kind of sound by dragging your wet finger across the rim of a glass.

GLUE STICK

What Causes Glue to Stick?

MATERIALS

glue
2 small pieces of paper

PROCEDURE

1. Glue the small pieces of paper together.
2. Let them dry for a few minutes, then shake the pieces of paper.

EXPLANATION

The pieces of paper stuck together. They held together because of the molecules in the glue. The protein molecules in the glue provided a bridge between the surfaces.

GETAWAY CAR

How Do Magnets Repel?

MATERIALS

2 bar magnets with N and S printed on them
masking tape
metal toy car

PROCEDURE

1. Stack the bar magnets so they stick together.
2. Take the bar magnets apart.
3. Tape one bar magnet to the car.
4. Hold the other bar magnet near the car. Experiment with moving the bar magnet so it will attract and repel the car. Watch the effect that opposite poles and same poles have on one another.

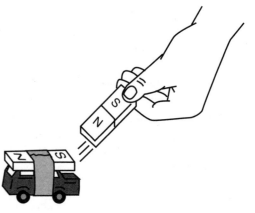

EXPLANATION

A **magnet** is a piece of iron or steel that attracts some metals. Every magnet has two ends or magnetic poles. These poles are north and south and point toward the direction of the earth's magnetic poles. The opposite poles of two magnets attract each other, but the same poles **repel** (push away) each other. When you pointed the north pole of one magnet at the north pole of the other magnet, the magnets repelled each other and the car moved away.

MAGNET PICK-UP

How Does a Magnet Magnetize Other Objects?

MATERIALS

3 very small metal cars
wand magnet

PROCEDURE

1. Place the cars on a table or other flat surface.
2. Hold the magnet near one metal car.
3. Pull the metal car with the magnet.
4. Position the first car near the second car. Get the cars close enough so that the second car sticks to the first when you hold the magnet near the first car.
5. Pull the 2 cars in a line with the magnet.
6. Try to pull the third car along with the others.

EXPLANATION

When you pulled one metal car, the other metal cars followed. Magnets attract metal objects with an invisible force. Before you held the magnet near the cars, the atoms inside each car were scattered, like pins that have fallen on the floor. When you placed the magnet near the car, the magnetic force rearranged the atoms in a straight line, causing the metal cars to become temporarily magnetized. This process continued until the force was so weak that it could not pass through any more metal cars.

MAGNET TOWER

In Which Direction Do Magnets Point?

MATERIALS

10 books of the same size
ruler
8-inch (20-cm) piece of string
bar magnet
compass

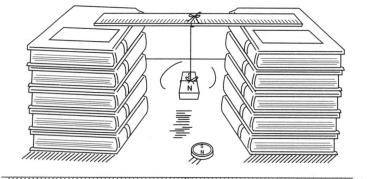

PROCEDURE

1. Stack 5 of the books on a table or other flat surface.

2. Make another stack of 5 books, leaving a 6-inch (15-cm) space between the two stacks of books.

3. Lay the ruler across the two stacks of books.

4. Tie the string around the magnet so that there is about 6 inches (15 cm) of string left free.

5. Tie the free end of the string to the center of the ruler so that the magnet hangs in the air between the stacks of books. The magnet will twist and twirl around, then come to a stop. Lay the compass on the table. Read the compass direction. Where is each end of the magnet facing?

6. Move the stacks of books so they face in another direction. Where do the ends of the magnet face now?

EXPLANATION

Each time the magnet stopped swinging, the north end of the magnet pointed north and the south end pointed south. Despite the position of the books, the magnet always pointed in the same direction. This is because the earth itself acts like a giant magnet. The poles of the bar magnet line up with the earth's **magnetic field** (the area in which a magnetic force is in effect).

42

COMPASS CONFUSION

What Effect Does a Bar Magnet Have on a Compass?

MATERIALS

bar magnet
compass

Note: This activity can permanently damage the compass, so use an inexpensive one. Do not let the magnet touch the compass.

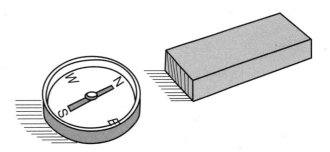

PROCEDURE

1. Lay the bar magnet on a table or other flat surface.
2. Place the compass near one end of the magnet. Read the compass.
3. Move the compass to the other end of the magnet. Read the compass.
4. Place the compass near the middle of the magnet. Read the compass.

EXPLANATION

Each time you read the compass, it pointed in a different direction, even though the earth's magnetic field remained constant. When a compass is near a bar magnet, the earth's magnetic field has little effect on the compass. The compass needle will line up instead with the bar magnet's magnetic field.

PUTTY PULL-UP

How Does Silly Putty® Pull a Cartoon from the Funny Pages?

MATERIALS

Silly Putty
newspaper

PROCEDURE

1. Press some Silly Putty into a flat piece.
2. Press the flattened Silly Putty onto a cartoon in the funny pages of the newspaper.
3. Lift the Silly Putty from the newspaper. Look at the Silly Putty.

EXPLANATION

The paper that comics are printed on is very thin. If regular ink were used to print on this paper, the ink would bleed right through. Instead printers use ink that sticks loosely to the paper. When you pressed the Silly Putty onto the paper, the ink was adsorbed by the Silly Putty. **Adsorption** occurs when a substance sticks to the surface of a material. The Silly Putty pulls the ink off the paper when you lift it off.

Note: If you press the Silly Putty, picture side down, onto a blank piece of paper, the picture will show up on the blank piece of paper.

ETCH-A-SKETCH®

How Does an Etch-A-Sketch Work?

MATERIALS

Etch-A-Sketch

PROCEDURE

1. Turn the knobs on the Etch-A-Sketch. Make any kind of shape you like.
2. Turn the Etch-A-Sketch upside down and shake it.
3. Turn the Etch-A-Sketch right side up again. What happens?

EXPLANATION

The picture you drew disappears. Behind the Etch-A-Sketch screen is a dustlike substance similar to graphite, the material used in pencil leads. The dust sticks to the screen because of **static electricity,** an electric charge that stays in one place rather than moves around to form an electric current. Static electricity occurs when two things rub together. This rubbing together causes the dust inside the Etch-A-Sketch to stick to the screen. The screen and the dust are attracted to one another enough to form a solid covering over the screen. When you draw on this covering, a little pointer inside pushes the dust away so you can see through. When you shake the Etch-A-Sketch, the dust stored inside is shaken around and sticks to the screen again. The dust covers your picture, so you can draw another one.

BALANCING, SWINGING, AND SPINNING

BLOCK CENTER

How Can Your Finger Demonstrate the Center of Gravity?

MATERIALS

long, thin block or ruler

PROCEDURE

1. Place your hand palm down on a table.
2. Keeping your hand on the table, lift your pointer finger.
3. Lay the block across your lifted finger. Without using your other hand, move the block back and forth until it balances.

EXPLANATION

The block balanced across your finger if you put the block in the right spot. The spot at which it balanced is called the **center of gravity.** The center of gravity is that point where an object balances perfectly. The force of gravity was pulling down equally on both sides of the block, so the block balanced perfectly.

TALL TOWER

How Can You Make a Taller Block Building?

MATERIALS

set of building blocks

PROCEDURE

1. Make a pile of short blocks and one of long blocks.
2. On a table or other flat surface, build a tower as high as you can with short blocks first. Stack the blocks end to end. How high can you go before it falls?
3. Build a tower using long blocks and go as high as possible. Which tower was higher before it fell over?

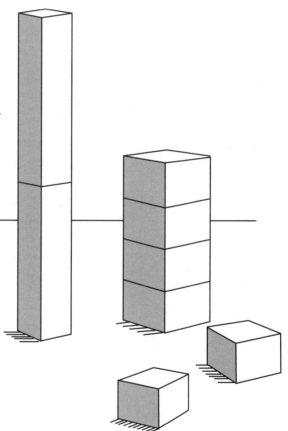

EXPLANATION

The tower made of long blocks was higher. In order for a tower to balance, you want the balance point (or center of gravity) as far from the edge of the tower as possible. A tall, skinny tower made with long blocks has a balance point that is very close to the edge. A fatter tower made with short blocks has a balance point that is farther from the edge. It is very easy to tip over a tall, skinny tower, but a fat tower is much harder to tip over.

SYMMETRICAL BUILDINGS

What Makes an Object Symmetrical?

MATERIALS

building blocks

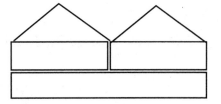

PROCEDURE

1. Find 2 long blocks that are exactly alike.
2. Lay the long blocks end to end on a table or other flat surface.
3. Find 2 triangular blocks that are exactly alike and place one on top of each of the long blocks so that their pointed ends face upward like housetops.
4. Look at the block structure. Remove one of the triangular blocks and look again.

EXPLANATION

An object has **symmetry** if it has two sides that are mirror images. To determine whether something is symmetrical, draw an imaginary line down the center of the object. If it looks the same on both sides, it is symmetrical. (If you were to draw a line down the center of your body, you would find that your body is symmetrical.)

Note: The blocks looked like mirror images until one of the triangular blocks was removed.

STAYING PUT

What Effect Does Inertia Have on Objects?

MATERIALS

5 blocks of the same size
mallet

PROCEDURE

1. Stack the blocks neatly on a table or other flat surface.
2. Use the mallet to quickly strike the bottom block. What happens?

EXPLANATION

When you quickly struck the bottom block, the block that you hit moved, but the blocks on top of it stayed in place. This is because of inertia. **Inertia** is the tendency of an object to stay at rest unless an outside force acts upon it. The moving force of the mallet did not have time to spread to the other blocks. All of the force focused on the bottom block.

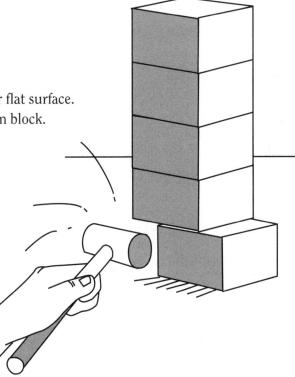

SEESAW BALANCE

How Does a Seesaw Balance?

MATERIALS

outdoor seesaw
friend who is about your size

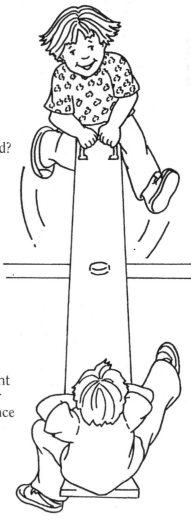

PROCEDURE

1. Sit on one end of the seesaw. What happens to the other end?
2. Ask a friend to sit on the other end. Be sure you and your friend sit an equal distance from the end of the seesaw.
3. Both of you should lift your legs slowly and try to balance the seesaw without using your legs to support your weight. Can you balance?
4. If you don't balance, have your friend move closer to the center of the seesaw, then try again to balance. Can you balance this way?
5. Stay in this position and try to seesaw up and down.

EXPLANATION

When you sat down on one end of the seesaw, the other end went up. When your friend sat on the other end, you went up. If your friend was about the same size as you, you could probably balance the seesaw easily. A seesaw is an example of a simple machine called a lever. A **lever** is a bar that turns on a point called the **fulcrum** to allow you to put extra force on something to lift it. You could not have picked your friend straight up off the ground, but with the lever you could lift him easily.

YO-YO BALANCE

How Does a Yo-Yo Work?

MATERIALS

yo-yo
masking tape
large washer

PROCEDURE

1. Play with the yo-yo on a flat surface.
2. Lay the yo-yo on a table, then tape the washer to one side of the yo-yo.
3. Try to get the yo-yo to work. What happens?

EXPLANATION

The yo-yo didn't work properly with the washer taped to one side. When your yo-yo goes up and down, it spins around a little hub in the middle. In order for a yo-yo or anything else to spin without wobbling, its weight has to be very carefully balanced. When you taped the washer to one side of the yo-yo, that side became different in weight from the other side. The yo-yo was no longer balanced, so it wobbled.

BLOCK BALANCE

How Can You Compare Weights?

MATERIALS

set of blocks
several small toys (such as cars or game pieces)

PROCEDURE

1. Find a medium-size square block and place it on the floor.
2. Find a very long block and lay it over the square block so that the long block balances.
3. Put a small block on one end of the long block. What happens?
4. Put the same kind of block on the other end of the long block. What happens?
5. Experiment by putting other blocks and small toys on the ends of the long block to see what happens.

EXPLANATION

You made a balance. A balance is a device used to compare the weights of objects by putting them at opposite ends of the balance. When objects that weighed the same were placed on either end of the long block (your balance), the long block stayed level. When the object on one end weighed more than the object on the other end, the long block tipped or fell toward one end.

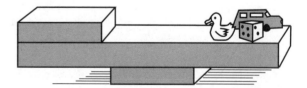

GRAVITY STACK

Why Don't Books Stacked over the Edge of a Table Fall?

MATERIALS

7 books of about the same size
ruler

PROCEDURE

1. Place 1 book on a table so that the edge of the book lines up with the edge of the table, and the spine (back) of the book faces the center of the table.

2. Place another book on the first book, but make it hang over the edge of the table about ½ inch (1.3 cm).

3. Place another book on the second book so that it extends past the edge of the table even farther than the second book.

4. Continue stacking the books until all of them are used. Adjust the positioning of the books as needed to be sure the books balance on the edge of the table.

EXPLANATION

The topmost book extends past the edge of the table, but it does not fall. This is because the center of gravity for the stack of books is where the entire weight of the books is concentrated. The center of gravity of all of the books remains on the table, so even the topmost book does not fall. You can disturb the center of gravity if you move the top book over the edge a little more. When you do this, it changes the center of gravity where the stack is balanced, and so the books will fall.

SWING PUMP

Why Does Pumping Your Legs Move a Swing?

MATERIALS

outdoor swing

PROCEDURE

1. Sit on the swing.
2. Try to move the swing without moving your legs. Can you move the swing very well?
3. Put your legs together and move them back and forth, pumping the swing. Can you go higher using your legs to pump?

EXPLANATION

When you pumped your legs, the swing went higher and higher. Gravity kept the swing returning to its lowest position. Pumping your legs put energy into the swing. The more you pumped, the more energy went into raising the swing higher.

MERRY-GO-ROUND MOVEMENT

Why Does a Merry-Go-Round Eventually Stop After It Is Pushed?

MATERIALS

merry-go-round
friend

PROCEDURE

1. Get on the merry-go-round.
2. Ask your friend to make the merry-go-round turn by pushing it a minute.
3. When your friend lets go, feel the movement of the merry-go-round. What happens after a few minutes?

EXPLANATION

When your friend pushed the merry-go-round, it moved quite fast. When the pushing stopped, the merry-go-round slowed down and eventually stopped. It stopped because of friction. There are two sources of friction for a merry-go-round: the air around it and the parts that allow it to turn. The friction slowly robbed the merry-go-round of the energy your friend put in it to make it go around. That made it slow down.

57

STOP TOP

Why Does the Base of a Top Move Around While It Is Spinning?

MATERIALS

spinning top

PROCEDURE

1. Spin the top and watch it move.
2. Without touching the top, let it come to a stop. Watch what happens when it stops.
3. Conduct the experiment several times to see if the same thing happens each time.

EXPLANATION

The top moved around the floor in wider and wider circles as it slowed down, until it eventually stopped and fell over. **Precession** is the gradual change in direction of the **axis** (a straight line around which something turns) of a spinning object. The axis of a spinning top moves in a circle. As the top slows down, the circle of precession gets larger and larger until the top finally falls over. A top that is not spinning will always fall on its side because of gravity.

PING-PONG™ POP

How Can You Keep a Ping-Pong Ball from Falling?

MATERIALS

Ping-Pong ball
jar without lid

PROCEDURE

1. Place the Ping-Pong ball on a table or other flat surface.
2. Put the jar upside down over the ball.
3. Hold the jar in your hand and start moving it in a circular motion. The ball should move around the inside walls of the jar and start climbing as the jar is swirled.
4. Continue swirling the jar and lift it off the table. What happens to the ball?

EXPLANATION

When you lifted the jar off the table, the ball stayed inside. The ball was held up because of **centrifugal force,** the force that tends to push outward on an object moving in a circle. When an object such as the ball is moving in a circle, this force tends to push the ball outward, so it continues moving in that manner.

CAR LOOP-OVER

Why Doesn't a Toy Car Fall Off a Looping Track When It Goes Upside Down?

MATERIALS

race car loop track
friction car

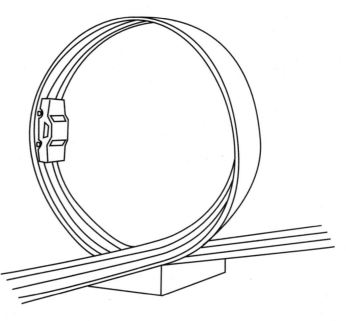

PROCEDURE

1. Build a track that loops, as shown in the illustration.
2. Rev the car wheels up several times.
3. Place the car on the track. What happens to the car when it is upside down on the track?

EXPLANATION:

Centrifugal force is the force that tends to push outward on an object moving in a circle. **Centripetal force** is pulling the car inward to keep it moving in a circle. With no forces acting upon it, the car would just go straight. But since the track is forcing the car to move in a circle, centrifugal force pushes back and keeps the car on track.

GYROSCOPE PULL

Why Does a Gyroscope Balance?

MATERIALS

gyroscope
12-inch (30-cm) piece of string

PROCEDURE

1. Place the gyroscope on a flat surface.
2. Wind the string around the axle of the gyroscope, as shown in the illustration.
3. Holding the gyroscope with one hand, pull the string sharply to unwind it. What happens?
4. Try balancing the gyroscope on different things, such as your finger.

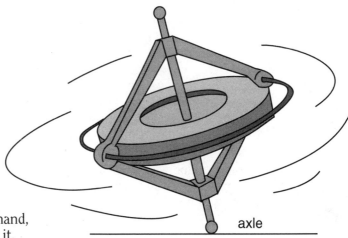

axle

EXPLANATION

A gyroscope is an instrument mounted on two rings that spins. When you pulled the string, the gyroscope started spinning and balanced on a point. A spinning object resists the force of gravity. It creates its own momentum, called **angular momentum** (the amount of force a moving object has). Angular momentum makes wheels like those on a bicycle continue turning in the same direction and position in which they have been moving.

HULA HOOP®

What Keeps a Hula Hoop Moving?

MATERIALS

masking tape
Hula Hoop

PROCEDURE

1. Wrap a piece of masking tape around one spot on the Hula Hoop.
2. Put the Hula Hoop around your waist and give it a spin. Move your body back and forth as you try to keep the hoop spinning. What do you notice about the tape?

EXPLANATION

You can see from the tape that the hoop turns all the way around your body. The Hula Hoop moves around your body using **oscillatory motion,** a circling motion around an object. As you continue to move your body, the Hula Hoop continues to move around your body. When you stop, the motion slows down and finally stops, and the Hula Hoop falls to the ground.

THROWING, FLYING, AND FALLING

CATCH IT

Do Some People Have Quicker Reaction Times Than Others?

MATERIALS

Nerf ball
toddler
friend

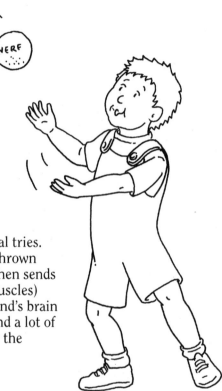

PROCEDURE

1. Throw the Nerf ball to a toddler. Try several times. Can the toddler catch it?
2. Throw the ball to a friend. Did your friend catch it?

EXPLANATION

The toddler probably did not catch the ball even after several tries. Your friend probably caught the ball easily. When a ball is thrown at you, your eyes send a message to your brain. The brain then sends the message through the nerves (fibers connecting your muscles) in your arms, hands, and fingers to catch the ball. Your friend's brain has had time to learn how to do this without having to spend a lot of time thinking about it. The toddler has not had the time or the experience to learn these reactions.

MOVE BACK

Why Does a Person Tend to Move Backward When Throwing a Ball?

MATERIALS

roller skates
basketball
outdoor area

PROCEDURE

1. Go outdoors and put your roller skates on.
2. Be ready to roll back. Toss the basketball.

EXPLANATION

As you threw the basketball forward away from you, the skates moved you in the opposite direction, backward. The English scientist Sir Isaac Newton described three laws of motion. By "laws" we mean the rules that we think nature obeys. His third law of motion was that for every action there is an equal and opposite reaction. You could feel this law of motion in action when you tossed the ball while wearing skates.

BALL TOSS

Which Goes Farther, a Light Ball or a Heavy Ball?

MATERIALS

small rubber ball
basketball
outdoor area
friend

PROCEDURE

1. Give your friend the rubber ball while you take the basketball.
2. Both you and your friend should throw the balls as far as you can. Which ball goes farther?
3. Now exchange balls and repeat step 2. What happens this time?

EXPLANATION

The small rubber ball went farther than the basketball no matter who threw it. When the force on two objects is the same, the lighter object will go farther than the heavy one, because the lighter object has less **mass** (the amount of matter in a material). More mass slows down the rate of motion. The lighter ball goes farther because it travels faster.

FOOTBALL FLIGHT

Why Should You Spin a Football When You Throw It?

MATERIALS

football
outdoor area

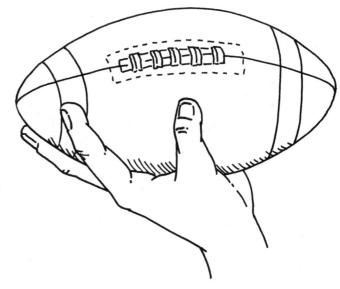

PROCEDURE

1. Hold the football by its middle.
2. Throw the ball straight. Watch it travel through the air. Does it fly straight or tumble through the air?
3. Hold the football by one end.
4. Throw the football with a spin. Watch it travel through the air. Does it fly straight or tumble?
5. Experiment with different ways to throw the football.

EXPLANATION

If a football is not spinning when you throw it, it will tumble rather than fly straight. A football's shape makes the ball go very far when you throw it correctly. The football must fly nose-first through the air. To stabilize the football in flight, the person throwing the ball must spin it. The ability to stabilize an object in flight by throwing it with a spin is called **gyroscopic stability.**

FLYING FRISBEE™

How Does a Frisbee Fly?

MATERIALS

Frisbee
outdoor area

PROCEDURE

1. Go outdoors and grasp the Frisbee in your hand with your thumb on top and your fingers curled underneath.
2. Quickly snap your wrist and let the Frisbee fly.

Low Pressure

High Pressure

Frisbee™

EXPLANATION

A Frisbee flies because it is curved in a certain way. As air passes over the curved upper surface of the Frisbee, the air speeds up. This faster air has lower pressure than the air under the Frisbee. The difference in air pressure makes the Frisbee go up. This upward force is called **lift.** The spinning motion generated from throwing the Frisbee stabilizes the Frisbee as it flies.

THROWING CURVES

Why Do Thrown Objects Make an Arc before Falling?

MATERIALS

Velcro darts or ball

PROCEDURE

1. Stand the suggested distance from the Velcro dartboard as recommended in the game directions.

2. Grasp a Velcro dart in your hand and toss it straight at the board.

3. Closely watch the Velcro dart as it flies through the air. What do you notice about the path of the Velcro dart?

4. Throw the dart again, this time aiming the dart slightly above the board. What happens?

EXPLANATION

When you threw the Velcro dart straight at the dartboard, it fell before reaching the board. To hit the dartboard, the dart had to be thrown at a point somewhere above the board. A dart goes up because of the force you put on it, then comes down because of gravity. The curved path that the dart makes in the air is its **trajectory.** The study of the movement of **projectiles** (objects thrown or driven forward) is called **ballistics.**

69

HELIUM HIGH

Why Does a Balloon Filled with Helium Float through the Air?

MATERIALS

piece of string about 3 feet (1 m) long
helium-filled balloon
several small toys
enclosed room

PROCEDURE

1. Tie the string to the helium-filled balloon.
2. In an enclosed room, let the balloon loose. Watch what happens.
3. Pull the balloon back and tie the free end of the string to one of your toys. Does the balloon still float to the ceiling?
4. Untie the toy from the balloon and choose another toy to tie to the string.
5. Continue testing the toys until you find one that keeps the helium-filled balloon from floating to the ceiling.

EXPLANATION

Without toys tied to it, the balloon floated upward till it was stopped by the ceiling. Helium is a gas that is lighter than air. A balloon filled with helium floats because it weighs less than the air around it. When you tied the toys to the string, they acted as weights. Heavy objects tied to the balloon weighed it down, so it no longer floated.

KITE FLYING

What Makes a Kite Fly?

MATERIALS

kite with string
open outdoor area

Note: This experiment should be performed on a windy day.

PROCEDURE

1. Unwind the string on the kite a few feet (meters).
2. Hold the kite above your head and behind you.
3. Run into the wind until the kite lifts up into the air.
4. When the kite is in the air, turn and stand with your back to the wind.
5. Unwind more string whenever the wind carries the kite farther into the air.
6. Rewind the string when the kite seems to be falling to the ground.
7. To stop the kite from flying, rewind the string and let the kite fall to the ground.

EXPLANATION

A kite flies because it is constructed to be angled in such a way that it meets the air with greater pressure on its front side than on its back. As with the curved Frisbee, the shape of the kite creates lift. When you pull on the string, the kite puts up more **resistance** (an opposing force) to the wind. This is known as **drag.** The shape, size, and construction of the kite help create lift and drag. But the design and construction of the kite are only part of the reason why the kite flies. The amount of wind, the strength of the materials, the kite's center of gravity, the weight, the length of the tail, and the amount of pull you use are other factors that help the kite to fly.

PAPER FLIGHT

Why Does a Paper Airplane Fly?

MATERIALS

sheet of typing paper

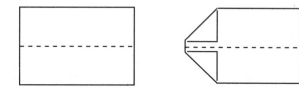

PROCEDURE

1. Fold the sheet of paper in half the long way.
2. Unfold the paper.
3. Fold the two corners of the short end of the paper down toward the center to touch the first fold.
4. Fold the long edges of the paper so that they touch the center fold.
5. Fold the paper in half the long way again, as you did in step 1.

6. Fold each side down to touch the center fold to make the plane's wings.
7. Hold the back of the plane and toss the plane into the air forward (nose-first). What happens?

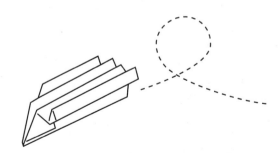

8. Now hold the front of the plane and throw it into the air backward (tail-first). How does it fly?

EXPLANATION

You made a paper airplane that flew when you threw it. The shape of the wings created lift. The air under the wings created drag, which pushed up on the wings to keep the plane from falling quickly. The pointed shape of the nose made the air move around the plane instead of hitting it head-on to stop its movement. Gravity eventually pulled the plane back to Earth.

BALLOON BLAST

JET PROPULSION

Why Does a Balloon Fly When You Let the Air Out of It?

MATERIALS

balloon

PROCEDURE

1. Blow the balloon all the way up.
2. Hold the neck of the balloon closed and move the balloon away from your face.
3. Let go of the neck of the balloon. What happens?

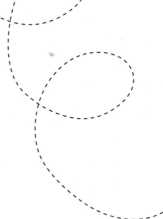

EXPLANATION

As the air came out of the balloon in one direction, the balloon flew in the other direction. The action of the air bursting out of one end of the balloon caused a reaction that pushed the balloon in the other direction. This thrust, called **jet propulsion,** is the driving force of a body or object by means of a jet of gas or liquid. It is the same kind of thrust that moves rocket ships.

OUTSIDE ORBIT

What Happens When Objects Are in Orbit?

MATERIALS

tennis ball
small, empty, mesh onion bag
3 feet (1 m) of string
outdoor area

PROCEDURE

1. Put the tennis ball in the onion bag.
2. Lace the string through the opening of the onion bag.
3. Close the bag and tie a large knot in one end of the string near the bag to hold the tennis ball in the bag.
4. Take the bagged ball outside.
5. Hold the free end of the string above your head and start pivoting your elbow to start the ball spinning. Watch the path of the ball.
6. Let go of the string. What happens?

EXPLANATION

The ball circles around your body. The string represents the force of gravity keeping the smaller object (the ball) revolving around the larger object (you). The path traced by an object as it goes around another body is an **orbit.** When you let the string go, the ball flew away from you. The ball was no longer kept in orbit by gravity.

HAIR DRYER HIGH

Can Air Hold Up a Ping-Pong Ball?

MATERIALS

blow-dryer
3 Ping-Pong balls
Note: Ask an adult for permission to use the blow-dryer.

PROCEDURE

1. Turn the blow-dryer on to the cool setting and point the nozzle upward.
2. Put a Ping-Pong ball in the blow-dryer's airstream.
3. Add another Ping-Pong ball to the airstream.
4. Add the third ball. Do all of the balls stay in the air?

EXPLANATION

The blow-dryer sends up a powerful force of air that holds up one or more Ping-Pong balls. The balls don't fall to either side of the airstream because of the difference in air pressure. The fast-moving airstream is surrounded by still air. The fast-moving airstream pushes outward with less pressure than the still air pushes inward. If a ball drifts toward the edge of the airstream, the still air pushes the ball back into it. All energy is conserved (saved). We cannot make energy or destroy it. We can change its form, however. By balancing and suspending the ball in the center of the airstream of the upturned blow-dryer, you experimented with a well-known law of physics called **Bernoulli's law.** This law states that the pressure exerted by a fluid decreases as the fluid speeds up. It allows airplanes to fly, rapidly spinning baseballs to curve, and Frisbees to sail a long distance.

SLINKY® DOWN

Why Does a Slinky Slink Down Steps?

MATERIALS

Slinky
steps

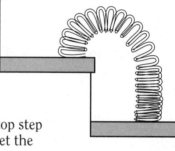

PROCEDURE

1. Place the Slinky at the top of the steps.
2. Bend the top few coils of the Slinky slightly over the top step so the Slinky begins to move down to the next step. Let the Slinky go. What happens?

EXPLANATION

When the Slinky was sitting flat on the top of a step, it had **potential energy** (stored energy). When you started the Slinky moving down the steps, you put some energy into it. You turned its potential energy into kinetic energy. The Slinky is a spring. Springs are very good at storing energy. As more of the spring went over each step, gravity also put energy into the spring. But once the spring started down the steps and gravity affected it, the potential energy was converted to the energy of motion, or kinetic energy, and the Slinky gracefully tumbled coil by coil down the steps. As the Slinky moved down the steps, energy was transferred along its length in a wave, which traveled through it by transferring energy.

PARACHUTE PLIGHT

How Does the Size of a Parachute Affect Its Fall?

MATERIALS

scissors
ruler
ball of string
large handkerchief

small handkerchief
2 identical small toys
high steps with a porch
    at the top

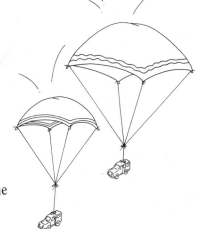

PROCEDURE

1. Use the scissors to cut 8 pieces of string about 10 inches (25 cm) long. Be sure all of the pieces are exactly the same length.
2. Tie 1 piece of string to each corner of the 2 handkerchiefs.
3. Gather the 4 strings of one handkerchief in the middle of the handkerchief and tie them in a knot. Do the same with the other handkerchief. You have made 2 parachutes.
4. Cut 2 pieces of string 6 inches (15 cm) long.
5. Use the 6-inch (15-cm) pieces of string to tie a toy to the knot of the string of each parachute.
6. Drop both parachutes from the porch at the same time. Which reaches the ground first?

EXPLANATION

The smaller parachute fell to the ground faster. A **parachute** is a device that slows the movement of objects falling through the air. The fall of a parachute is affected by two forces. Gravity is constantly pulling objects toward the center of the earth, and air is resisting gravity's force. The pull of gravity is much greater than air resistance (the opposing force of air), so air only slows the fall of the parachute rather than stops it. With its greater surface area, the larger parachute experienced more air resistance, so it was slower to fall.

MARBLE DROP

Which Hits the Floor First, an Object Moving Forward or One Falling Straight Down?

MATERIALS

2 marbles

PROCEDURE

1. Hold a marble in each hand.
2. At the same time, toss one marble forward and drop the other. Which marble hits the floor first?

EXPLANATION

The marbles landed on the floor at the same time. The force of gravity acts the same on falling objects whether they are moving forward or falling straight down.

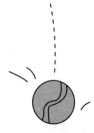

78

DOMINO DOWN

How Are Closely Placed Objects Affected When One Falls?

MATERIALS

box of dominoes
ruler

PROCEDURE

1. Stand one of the dominoes on end on a table or other flat surface.
2. Stand another domino on end about ½ inch (1.25 cm) from the first domino.
3. Continue standing dominoes on end until you have formed a line. The line can be curved, as long as each domino will be able to knock the next one over.
4. After all of the dominoes have been arranged, tap the first domino lightly. What happens? What do you think would happen if you could put a million dominoes in line?

EXPLANATION

Each domino has energy. If knocked over, it has a little less energy, because the middle of the domino is a little closer to the ground. The balance point is different when the domino is standing on its edge as opposed to when it is lying flat. Imagine how your balance point is different when you are standing as opposed to when you are lying down. The energy that the domino has when it's standing is called potential energy. When the domino begins to fall, it has less potential energy and more kinetic energy, which is moving energy. You provided the little bit of energy needed to knock the first one down, then the energy it lost in falling down was used to knock the next one down. This went on for as many dominoes as you had lined up.

MARBLE RUN

How Can Gravity Be Made to Do Work?

MATERIALS

marble game such as Super Cascade

PROCEDURE

1. Examine the pieces of the marble run game.
2. Design the marble course. Be sure to add the paddle wheels, chutes, and bridges so the marbles will travel through them.
3. Put the marble at the top of the racecourse, let it go, and watch what happens.

EXPLANATION

You constructed a structure that put gravity to work. When you let the marble go at the top of the racecourse, gravity pulled it through passageways, made it turn paddle wheels, and pulled it over bridges. You used gravity's action on the marble to make things happen.

FLOATING, BOUNCING, AND PUSHING

WATER TOYS

Why Do Some Objects Sink and Others Float?

MATERIALS

miscellaneous waterproof toys
bathtub or sink

PROCEDURE

1. Place the toys in the bathtub.
2. Put the stopper in the drain and turn the water on slowly. Watch what happens to the toys as the water fills the bathtub.

EXPLANATION

As the water rose in the bathtub, some of the toys began to float, while the others stayed at the bottom. The objects that floated to the top were more buoyant than the ones that remained on the bottom. **Buoyancy** is the upward force exerted on an object by a liquid such as water. When an object is buoyant, it floats in a liquid. The toys that floated pushed aside an equal amount of water that was pushing upward on them. The toys that pushed less water out of the way did not have enough upward force to float, so they stayed at the bottom.

CLAY BOAT

Why Do Toy Boats Float?

MATERIALS

small piece of clay
large bowl of water

PROCEDURE

1. Roll the clay into a ball.
2. Put the ball of clay in the bowl of water. What happens to the ball of clay?
3. Remove the ball of clay from the water.
4. Form the same piece of clay into a boat shape.
5. Put the clay boat in the water. What happens?

EXPLANATION

The clay ball sank to the bottom of the water, but the clay boat floated. Boats float because of buoyancy. The buoyant force is equal to the amount of water **displaced** (moved out of position). When you flattened the clay, the shape was changed enough to also change the amount of water displaced out of position. The amount of water displaced weighed more than the flattened clay, so it floated. When the clay was a ball, the displaced water weighed less and so the ball sank.

FLOATING TUBE

Why Does a Tube Full of Air Help a Person Float?

MATERIALS

inner tube
swimming pool or beach

*Note: Be sure the pool or beach allows inner tubes and
is supervised by a lifeguard.*

PROCEDURE

1. Walk into the water until it is about chest high.
2. Lift your feet off the ground. Can you float?
3. Come out of the water, then put the inner tube around
   your waist.
4. Walk into the water again and repeat step 2.

EXPLANATION

When you first went into the water without the tube, you could
not float. But when the inner tube was around your waist, you
were able to float. The ability of an object to float is due to
buoyancy. The inner tube floats because it is full of air, which
is much lighter than water.

SMALL ON TOP

How Can the Energy of One Ball Be Transferred to Another?

MATERIALS

basketball
tennis ball
outdoor area

PROCEDURE

1. Hold the basketball in one hand.
2. Hold the tennis ball on top of the basketball.
3. Without using any force on either ball, release both of the balls at the same time. What happens?

EXPLANATION

When you dropped the basketball with the tennis ball on top of it, the basketball bounced a little, but the tennis ball shot high into the air. When the balls hit the ground together, some of the energy that normally would lift the basketball was transferred from the basketball to the tennis ball.

BALL BOUNCE

Do a Large Ball and a Small Ball Use the Same Amount of Energy When Bouncing?

MATERIALS

basketball
tennis ball
outdoor area

PROCEDURE

1. Hold the basketball in one hand and the tennis ball in your other hand.
2. Drop the balls at the same time, being sure not to use any force.

EXPLANATION

Gravity is always pulling on objects. When you let go of the balls, gravity pulled them both to the ground. Both balls bounced back to about the same height, but more energy was needed for the basketball to reach the same height as the tennis ball. The basketball had a greater mass than the tennis ball, so it needed more energy to move. Objects with more mass require more energy to move.

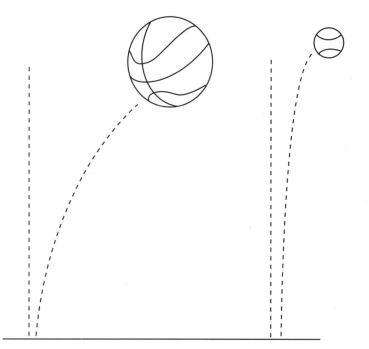

POGS 'N' SLAMMERS

Why Do Objects Sometimes Flip Over When They Are Hit?

MATERIALS

coin
pogs
2 or more players

PROCEDURE

1. Flip the coin to see who goes first.
2. Have each player count out the same number of pogs. Place these pogs in a stack, picture side down, on the ground.
3. The first player throws the piece called the "slammer" at the stack, trying to flip over as many of the pogs as possible.
4. The first player then gets to keep any pogs that landed picture side up. Any pogs that landed picture side down are put back in the stack.
5. The next player takes a turn throwing the slammer at the stack, trying to flip over as many of the pogs as possible.
6. Continue taking turns until the last pog is flipped over.

EXPLANATION

Pogs are pieces of cardboard about $1\frac{1}{2}$ inches (4 cm) in diameter, printed with pictures and/or words. The first pogs were made from caps covering the mouths of glass milk bottles. A slammer comes with every package of Pogs 'n' Slammers. It is the pog that is thrown at others to make them turn over. The pogs on the ground were storing energy, potential energy. When the slammer hit the stack of pogs, it exerted enough energy to bounce up. This caused the potential energy to change to kinetic energy, the energy of a moving object. Whether the pog then fell over one way or another was mostly due to chance, just like when you flip a coin.

JACK-IN-THE-BOX

How Does a Jack-in-the-Box Work?

MATERIALS

jack-in-the-box

PROCEDURE

1. Be sure the jack is in the box.
2. Turn the crank to make the jack pop out of the box.

EXPLANATION

When you pushed the jack down into the box, you gave it potential energy. When you turned the crank, a mechanism caused the lid of the box to pop open. The potential energy of the jack was converted to kinetic energy, which pushed the jack out of the box.

ELECTRIC RECORD

How Can You Make Cereal Jump?

MATERIALS

puffed cereal
cereal bowl
old long-playing record
wool mitten

PROCEDURE

1. Place the puffed cereal in the bowl.
2. Rub the record with the wool mitten.
3. Hold the edge of the record above the puffed cereal. What happens?

EXPLANATION

The cereal jumped up and down in the bowl. All matter is made up of tiny atoms, which in turn contain even smaller particles called **electrons** (tiny bits of electricity). Electrons have negative electric charges. Rubbing the record with the mitten transferred electrons from the mitten to the record. This gave the record a negative charge. When you held the record over the cereal, the negative charge attracted the positive charges in the cereal. When the cereal touched the record, the electrons on the record were transferred to the cereal. The cereal and the record both then had the same negative charge, so they repelled each other. The cereal seemed to jump up and down. The electric charge you created this way is called static electricity, which is a form of electricity in which the electric charge remains motionless rather than flowing in a current.

PINWHEEL POWER

Does the Wind Have Power?

MATERIALS

toy pinwheel
outdoor area

Note: This experiment should be performed on a windy day.

PROCEDURE

1. Take the pinwheel outside on a windy day.
2. Hold it in the wind. What happens?

EXPLANATION

The wind made the pinwheel turn. The wind's energy can be captured in windmills and made to do work. The turning windmills are attached to machines that can do many things, from grinding grains to generating electricity.

WATER SQUIRT

What Causes the Water to Squirt from a Water Gun?

MATERIALS

water gun
water

PROCEDURE

1. Fill the water gun with water.
2. Press the trigger (or press the side of the gun if there is no trigger). What happens?

EXPLANATION

When you squeezed the trigger of the water gun, you exerted pressure on the water inside. Pressure is the force exerted on a surface. The water reacted to the pressure to find a way to escape. The escape route of the water was through the tiny hole at the end of the water gun. Because the hole was so small, the water didn't come out until great pressure was put on it. When it eventually came out, the water then squirted some distance.

SUPER SOAKER™

Why Do Some Water Squirters Have a Pump on Them?

MATERIALS

Super Soaker
water
outdoor area with dry
    pavement

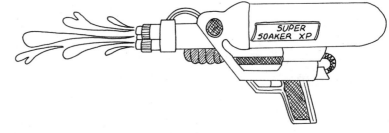

PROCEDURE

1. Fill the Super Soaker with water.
2. Pump the Super Soaker five times.
3. Aim the Super Soaker at a place on the pavement far away from you and shoot.
4. Pump the Super Soaker 15 times and aim it at a place near the area you wet before. Could you shoot the water farther this time?

EXPLANATION

When you pumped the Super Soaker 15 times, you were able to shoot the water farther. The pumping created more pressure inside the Super Soaker. The more pressure, the farther the water shot. Hydraulic machines get their power from the pressure of liquids. **Hydraulics** is the branch of science that deals with power generated from water pressure. The Super Soaker is a hydraulic machine.

EASY UP

What Is Pneumatics?

MATERIALS

3 or 4 books
small plastic bag

PROCEDURE

1. Place the plastic bag on a table.
2. Place the books on top of the bag, but be sure to leave the open end of the bag clear of the books.
3. Gather the ends of the bag together and blow into the bag. What happens to the books?

EXPLANATION

When you blew air into the plastic bag, you inflated the bag, which lifted the books. This is an example of **pneumatics,** in which a machine works because of compressed air. Pneumatics (the branch of physics dealing with the mechanical properties of air and other gases) is used in jackhammers as well as in the brakes of some large trucks.

93

WAVE CARDS

Why Does Dropping a Stone in a Pond Make the Water Ripple?

MATERIALS

deck of playing cards

PROCEDURE

1. Lay one card on a table.
2. Lay another card on the first card, leaving ¼ inch (0.65 cm) of the first card showing under the top card.
3. Continue laying the remaining cards on top of the others in a similar fashion until all of the cards are used.
4. Using your finger, gently lift the bottom card a little bit. Now move the card up and down, but do not flip the cards over.

EXPLANATION

When you pushed the bottom card up, it made a wavelike motion that spread through the line of cards. This is similar to the ripples you create when you throw a pebble into a calm body of water. The energy from the splash moves out through the water in little waves, but the water molecules actually only move up and down, like the cards.

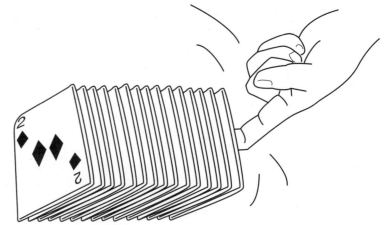

94

BICYCLE PEDALING

What Makes a Bicycle Move?

MATERIALS

bicycle
outdoor area
friend

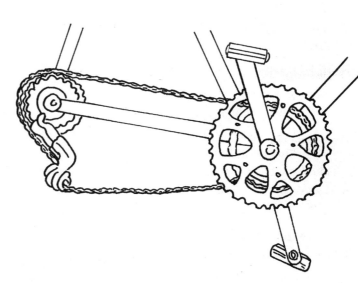

PROCEDURE

1. Study the chain and the pedals of the bicycle.

2. Have your friend get on the bicycle and ride while you observe the chains and pedals working together.

3. Ask your friend to change gears while you continue observing. What do you notice about the mechanism?

EXPLANATION

Between the pedals of the bicycle you noticed a chain connecting several **gears** (toothed wheels that turn to move a machine) to the back wheel of the bicycle. The different-sized gears in a bicycle control the number of times a person must pedal in order for the bicycle's back wheel to turn. Turning the large gear is harder, but makes the bike go farther with each push. This gear is best for downhill riding. Turning the small gear is easier, but it is necessary to pedal more times to go the same distance.

HOT PUMP

Why Does a Bicycle Pump Feel Hot After It Is Used?

MATERIALS

bicycle pump
flat bicycle tire

PROCEDURE

1. Unscrew the cap of the bicycle tire and set the cap in a place where it will not get lost.
2. Attach the nozzle of the bicycle pump to the tire nozzle.
3. Pump enough air in the tire to fill it.
4. Feel the bicycle pump. How does it feel?
5. Replace the cap of the bicycle tire.

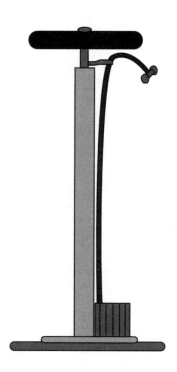

EXPLANATION

After pumping air into the tire of your bicycle, the pump felt hot. When you pumped air into the tire, the air molecules inside the pump were **compressed** (forced closer together). As the air molecules were forced together, they collided with each other and with the walls of the pump. The friction of the air molecules against the walls of the pump produced heat.

PLUCKING, BANGING, AND BLOWING

BANJO BOX

How Does the Width of a Banjo's Strings Affect Its Sound?

MATERIALS

2 rubber bands of different widths
1 large block, about 4×1 inch (10×2.5 cm)
2 cylindrical (can-shaped) blocks

PROCEDURE

1. Wrap the rubber bands around the length of the long block.

2. Slip one cylinder under both rubber bands at each end of the long block. This will lift the rubber bands above the block.

3. Pluck the rubber bands one at a time.

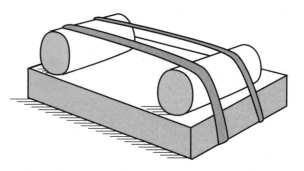

EXPLANATION

Sound is made by vibrating objects that send sound waves through the air to your ear. Sound waves travel through the air. When you plucked the rubber bands, they vibrated and made waves through the air that reached your ear. The thinner rubber band vibrated faster to make a higher note. The thicker rubber band vibrated slower to make a lower note.

PIANO PLAY

What Happens When a Piano Key Is Pressed?

MATERIALS

piano

PROCEDURE

1. Look inside the piano. What do you see?
2. Press one of the keys on the piano while you are looking inside. What happens?

EXPLANATION

A piano is a stringed instrument, like a guitar, only the strings are inside. When you pressed the piano key, it moved a hammer which in turn hit one of the piano wires. The piano wire vibrated and made a sound.

PIANO KEYS

Why Do Different Piano Keys Make Different Sounds?

MATERIALS

piano

PROCEDURE

1. Press one of the keys at one end of the keyboard.
2. Press a key at the opposite end of the keyboard. What is the difference in the sound?
3. Look inside the piano as you press the same keys again. What differences can you see between the strings making the notes?

EXPLANATION

One key produced a very high note, and the other a very low note. Two differences in the strings made the notes different: thickness and looseness. The thick string made a low note because it vibrated more slowly than the thin string. The thick string was also strung more loosely than the thin string. Loose strings give a lower sound than tight strings. To tune the piano and get the notes just right, a tuner turns the posts that the strings are attached to so that the strings become tighter or looser.

GUITAR HOLE

Why Does a Guitar Have a Hole in the Middle of It?

MATERIALS

acoustic guitar
masking tape

PROCEDURE

1. Pluck a string on the guitar. What kind of a sound does it make?
2. Completely tape over the sound hole of the guitar.
3. Now pluck the string again. How do the sounds differ?

EXPLANATION

Plucking the string made it vibrate, which produced sound. When you plucked the string, the vibrations traveled through the sound hole in the center of the guitar to vibrate the air inside the guitar. This made the sound of the string louder. When you covered up the sound hole with tape, the vibrations could not travel through the opening and the sound was much softer.

GOOD VIBRATIONS

Why Does My Radio Vibrate When It Is Playing?

MATERIALS

radio

PROCEDURE

1. Turn on the radio and turn the volume up.
2. Put your hand on the radio. What do you feel?

EXPLANATION

You felt the radio vibrating back and forth. The sound vibrations from the speakers in the radio travel through the casing, making it vibrate as well. Slow vibrations make low sounds, and fast vibrations make high sounds. These sound vibrations travel through the air to reach your ears. Inside your ear, they vibrate your eardrum. Your brain translates the vibrations into sounds.

DRUM VIBES

Does It Matter How Hard You Hit a Drum?

MATERIALS

drum
drumstick

PROCEDURE

1. Strike the drum hard, then feel the head of the drum.
2. Tap the drum lightly. Feel the head of the drum again. What do you notice about the vibrations and sound?

EXPLANATION

The drumhead vibrated when you hit it. When you struck the drum hard, you felt strong vibrations and heard a loud sound. When you tapped the drum lightly, the drum vibrations were weak and a very faint sound was produced.

DRUMBEAT

How Do Drums Make Different Sounds?

MATERIALS

drumsticks
several differently sized drums

PROCEDURE

Use the drumsticks to strike the center of each drum. How are the sounds different?

EXPLANATION

Larger drums will make lower, louder sounds and smaller drums will make higher, softer sounds. When you hit the drum with the drumstick, you caused the skin of the drum to vibrate. These vibrations were amplified by the air inside the drum. The larger the drum, the more air and skin that was vibrated, and the lower and louder the sound.

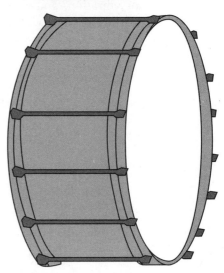

WHISTLE WONDER

What Purpose Does the Ball Serve in a Whistle?

MATERIALS

whistle

PROCEDURE

1. Examine the whistle. What are the parts of the whistle?
2. Put the whistle in your mouth and blow it.
3. Try to make different high and low sounds.

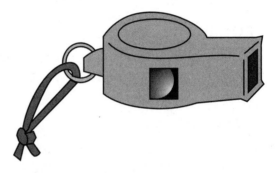

EXPLANATION

A whistle is an instrument that uses your breath to make sound. The air that you blew into the whistle passed across a slot, which caused the air inside the whistle to vibrate. The vibrating air made a sound that your ear could hear. The ball inside the whistle interfered with the vibrating air so that the sound's loudness and **pitch** (the high or low quality of sound) changed. These changes catch people's attention much more than a constant sound would. New whistles are using two balls to make two sounds at one time.

RECORDER READING

How Do You Make Different Sounds on a Recorder?

MATERIALS

recorder

PROCEDURE

1. Without covering any holes, blow in the recorder to make a sound.
2. Now hold your fingers over all of the holes and blow. How do the sounds differ?

EXPLANATION

The recorder is a woodwind instrument. Woodwind instruments use a column of air vibrating inside a tube to make sound. You changed the sound of the note by placing your fingers over the vibrating air column. Depending on the length of the air column, it **resonates** (reflects sound) at a certain frequency. Uncovering one or more holes along the tube shortens the column of vibrating air by letting some leak out of other holes. A shorter column of air resonates at a higher frequency, so you hear a higher-pitched tone.

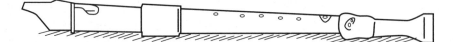

BIRTHDAY HORN

What Causes a Horn to Make a Sound?

MATERIALS

birthday party horn

PROCEDURE

1. Examine the horn's shape.
2. Blow the horn.

EXPLANATION

A horn is a tube filled with air that vibrates to make a sound when you blow through the reed into the mouthpiece. The horn gets wider toward the bottom and ends in a flare. The flare amplifies the sound coming out of the horn.

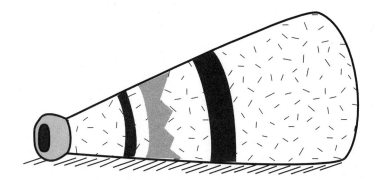

BELL SOUND

What Happens When a Bell Rings?

MATERIALS

bell

PROCEDURE

Move the bell until it clangs. What makes this sound?

EXPLANATION

The clapper of the bell hit the metal side of the bell, and the metal vibrated, producing sound. When a bell vibrates, the air around it also vibrates. The shape of the bell amplifies the sound. A small bell makes a little tinkle, but a huge bell, such as in a church, makes a sound that can be heard for miles (kilometers).

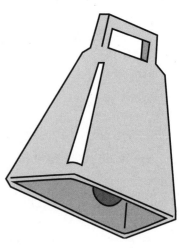

XYLOPHONE SUBSTITUTE

How Does a Xylophone Make Sound?

MATERIALS

4 identical glasses
water
ruler
wooden spoon

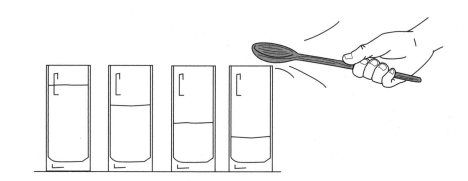

PROCEDURE

1. Place the glasses in a row on a table.
2. Fill the first glass three-fourths full with water.
3. Fill the remaining glasses so that each has about 1 inch (2.5 cm) less water than the one before it.
4. Tap each of the glasses with the wooden spoon and listen to the sounds.

EXPLANATION

When you hit the glasses with the spoon, you made musical sounds. When you hit the fullest glass, it made the lowest tone because the greater amount of water caused the glass to vibrate more slowly than the smaller amounts of water in the other glasses. A xylophone uses this principle with different materials. Pieces of wood or metal cut in different lengths make different sounds. The shorter pieces make higher notes because they vibrate faster.

109

SOUND WAVE

What Is Frequency?

MATERIALS

jump rope
ruler
friend

PROCEDURE

1. Hold one end of the rope and have your friend hold the other.

2. Stretch the rope between you, then let it drop down so it is about 2 inches (5 cm) from the ground.

3. Raise your hand above your head while your friend holds the other end of the rope still.

4. Snap the rope down quickly, and watch the waves move up and down toward your friend.

5. Ask your friend to snap the other end while you hold your end still. Watch the waves.

6. Make the rope move fast and slow, and study its movement.

EXPLANATION

When you moved the rope up and down, you created a series of waves. Sound moves through the air in waves. The rate of motion of the sound wave is measured in frequency. (Frequency is measured by the distance between the peaks of each wave.) Low frequencies have large distances between peaks and sound low. High frequencies have short distances between peaks and sound high.

COMPRESSION SLINKY®

How Do Sound Waves Work?

MATERIALS

Slinky
friend

PROCEDURE

1. Lay the Slinky on its side on a table or other flat surface.
2. Ask your friend to grasp one end of the Slinky while you grasp the other.
3. Stretch the Slinky loosely across the table.
4. Jerk your end suddenly toward your friend. What happens?

EXPLANATION

When you jerked the Slinky, you saw groups of coils springing back and forth. This looked like sound waves traveling through the air. When you hit a drum, it vibrates. Each time the drum vibrates, it sends a wave of vibrations through the air. When a drum approaches you at a parade, its sound waves are bunched up in front of the drum as they reach your ear. This creates a high-pitched sound. As the drum passes and goes away from you, the sound waves behind it are more stretched out. These waves reach your ears less frequently and the sound is lower pitched.

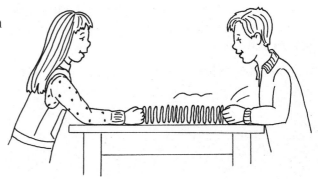

SPOKE CARDS

What Is the Doppler Effect?

MATERIALS

bicycle
playing card
spring-type clothespin
duct tape
friend

PROCEDURE

1. Turn the bicycle upside down.
2. Clip the playing card in the clothespin.
3. Position the card on one of the forks of the bicycle (the area of the bicycle that holds the wheel) so that the card hits one of the spokes of the bicycle wheel.
4. Tape the handle of the clothespin to the fork.
5. Move the wheel slowly so the spoke hits the card. Listen to the sound the card makes.
6. Ask your friend to ride the bicycle away from you, back to you, then past you at a constant speed. How does the sound of the spoke card change?

EXPLANATION

The sound was first lower, then higher, then lower again. When you hear a sound such as a siren approaching you, the sound gets not only louder, as you would expect, but also higher. This is known as the **Doppler effect.** As the object making the sound gets closer to you, the sound waves get closer together. This makes the frequency increase or decrease according to the speed at which the distance is increasing or decreasing. As the object moves away from you, the sound waves get farther apart and the pitch of the sound is lower again.

TAPE RECORDINGS

Why Does Your Voice Sound Different on a Tape Recording?

MATERIALS

blank cassette tape
cassette tape recorder
friend

PROCEDURE

1. Put the cassette tape in the tape recorder.
2. Press the Record button and ask your friend to talk, then take a turn talking.
3. Rewind the tape and listen to the voices. How do the taped voices compare to your actual voices?

EXPLANATION

When you talk, the sound waves move through the bone cavity of your head. This makes your voice sound lower in your ear. When you listen to your voice on tape, it does not go through this cavity, so it sounds higher. The tape recording is actually how your friend hears your voice.

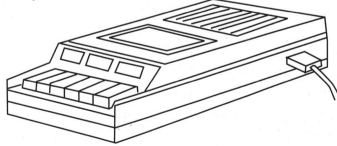

Glossary

acid: a chemical compound that dissolves in water and tastes sour.

adsorption: the sticking of a substance to the surface of a material.

angular momentum: the amount of force a moving object has.

axis: a straight line around which something turns.

ballistics: the study of the movement of projectiles.

Bernoulli's law: a physics law that states that the pressure exerted by a fluid decreases as the fluid speeds up.

buoyancy: the upward force exerted on an object by a liquid.

calcium carbonate: a somewhat soft, white, fine-grained substance that forms on the bottom of seas and that is mostly composed of seashells.

camouflage: the capability of some animals to match the background color to be less visible.

center of gravity: the point at which the force of gravity pulls down equally on both sides of an object, so that the object balances.

centrifugal force: the force that tends to push outward on an object moving in a circle.

centripetal force: the force that pulls inward to keep an object moving in a circle.

chemical bonds: connections between molecules.

chromatography: method of separating colors from paints through filter paper.

circuit: the complete path of an electric current.

compress: to reduce the volume of a material by pressure.

convex lenses: pieces of glass that are thicker in the middle than at the edges.

cornea: the outer layer of the eye.

displace: to move out of position.

Doppler effect: a change in sound waves so that the frequency increases or decreases according to the speed at which the distance is decreasing or increasing.

drag: the force that slows an object as it travels through a liquid or gas.

elastic: having the ability to easily stretch and return to the original shape.

electrons: tiny bits of electricity.

evaporation: the process by which a liquid changes into a gas.

force: the push or pull on an object.

friction: the force that acts when two surfaces rub against one another.

fulcrum: the point on which a lever turns.

gears: toothed wheels that turn to move a machine.

gravity: the force of attraction between any two objects that have mass.

gyroscopic stability: the ability to stabilize an object in flight by throwing it with a spin.

helium: a tasteless, colorless, odorless gas that is lighter than air.

hydraulics: the branch of science that deals with power generated from the pressure of water and other liquids.

inertia: the tendency of an object to stay at rest unless an outside force acts upon it.

jet propulsion: the driving force of an object by means of a jet of gas or other liquid.

kaleidoscope: a long, tubular instrument containing several mirrors that cause multiple reflections.

kinetic energy: the energy of a moving object.

latex: a gooey natural substance used to make elastic materials like balloons.

lever: a simple machine used for lifting a weight by pressing or pulling a bar that turns on a fulcrum.

lift: an upward force that results when the air pressure below a flying object is greater than the air pressure above it.

limestone: a rock containing calcium carbonate.

magnet: a piece of iron or steel that attracts certain kinds of metals.

magnetic field: an area in which a magnetic force is in effect.

magnification: the process of making an object look larger by passing light from it through a lens.

magnifying lens: a piece of glass that makes objects look larger.

mass: the amount of matter in a material.

molecule: the smallest part of a substance that has all the properties of the substance.

Mylar: a man-made polyester material made of very thin sheets.

non-Newtonian fluid: a fluid that behaves in some ways like a liquid and in other ways like a solid.

orbit: the path of one body around another body.

oscillatory motion: a circling motion around an object.

parachute: a device that slows the movement of objects falling through the air.

periscope: a tube-shaped instrument having lenses and mirrors by which to get a view that would otherwise be blocked.

phosphorescent: materials that give off light energy after being exposed to energy.

pigments: chemicals that absorb some wavelengths of light and reflect others, which you see as colors.

pitch: the high or low quality of sound.

pneumatics: the branch of science that deals with moving or working things by the pressure of air and other gases.

polymers: plastics made of long chains of molecules.

potential energy: stored energy.

precession: the gradual change in direction of the axis of a spinning object.

pressure: the force placed on an object.

primary colors: red, blue, and yellow.

prism: a piece of triangular transparent material that separates white light into different colors.

projectile: an object thrown or driven forward.

reflect: to bounce light back from objects.

refract: to bend light rays.

repel: to push away.

resistance: an opposing force.

resonate: to reflect sound.

retina: the inner layer of lining of the eyeball that reacts to light.

soluble: able to dissolve in water.

spectrum: a series of colored bands formed when light rays are broken up.

static electricity: an electric charge that stays in one place rather than moves around to form an electric current.

stereoscope: an instrument that combines two slightly different pictures of the same object to make it look three-dimensional.

stereoscopic vision: the ability of the brain to put two pictures together to see a three-dimensional image.

streamlining: positioning an object to reduce drag.

surface tension: the force by which water molecules cling together at the surface.

symmetry: the property by which a form or object looks exactly the same on both sides of an imaginary line drawn down the center.

trajectory: the curved path of an object flying through the air.

wavelength: the direction of movement of a wave.

Further Reading

Barr, George. *Science Projects for Young People* (New York: Little, Brown & Co., 1988).

Chapman, Philip. *The Usborne Young Scientist: Electricity* (Tulsa, Okla.: Educational Development Corp., 1991).

Churchill, E. Richard. *How to Make Optical Illusion Tricks and Toys* (New York: Sterling, 1989).

Doherty, Paul, Don Rahjen, and the Exploratorium Teacher Institute. *The Magic Wand and Other Experiments on Light and Color* (New York: John Wiley & Sons, 1995).

Falk, John. *Bubble Monster and Other Science Fun* (Chicago, Ill.: Chicago Review Press, 1997).

Kohl, MaryAnn. *Mudworks* (Bellingham, Wash.: Bright Ring, 1989).

Kohl, MaryAnn, and Jean Potter. *Science Arts* (Bellingham, Wash.: Bright Ring, 1994).

Mathieu, W. A. *The Listening Book: Discovering Your Own Music* (Boston, Mass.: Shambhala Publications, 1991).

Potter, Jean. *Nature in a Nutshell* (New York: John Wiley & Sons, 1995).

Potter, Jean. *Science in Seconds* (New York: John Wiley & Sons, 1995).

The Usborne Introduction to Physics (Tulsa, Okla.: Educational Development Corp., 1991).

Woelfle, Gretchen. *The Wind at Work* (Chicago, Ill.: Chicago Review Press, 1997).

Activity Index